PASSWORD NOT!

"5x8 inch Internet Password Log Book with Large Print"

THIS BOOK BELONGS TO

____

____

____

SOFTWARE INFORMATION

Software: ______________________________
Purchase Date: _________________________
License Key: ___________________________

____

Software: ______________________________
Purchase Date: _________________________
License Key: ___________________________

____

Software: ______________________________
Purchase Date: _________________________
License Key: ___________________________

____

Software: ______________________________
Purchase Date: _________________________
License Key: ___________________________

____

Software: ______________________________
Purchase Date: _________________________
License Key: ___________________________

____

COMPUTER INFORMATION

Computer #1: _______________________

Model: _______________________________

Serial Number: ________________________

Purchase Date: ________________________

Warranty: _____________________________

Support: ______________________________

Notes: ________________________________

____

Computer #2: _______________________

Model: _______________________________

Serial Number: ________________________

Purchase Date: ________________________

Warranty: _____________________________

Support: ______________________________

Notes: ________________________________

____

Computer #3: _______________________

Model: _______________________________

Serial Number: ________________________

Purchase Date: ________________________

Warranty: _____________________________

Support: ______________________________

Notes: ________________________________

____

NETWORK INFORMATION #1

ISP Name:

Website:

Account Number:

Email:

Password:

Support:

Notes:

Modem/Router:

Model:

Serial Number:

Admin URL:

Username:

Password:

Notes:

SSID (WiFi Network Name):

Password:

Security Mode:

Notes:

NETWORK INFORMATION #2

ISP Name:

Website:

Account Number:

Email:

Password:

Support:

Notes:

Modem/Router:

Model:

Serial Number:

Admin URL:

Username:

Password:

Notes:

SSID (WiFi Network Name):

Password:

Security Mode:

Notes:

Website:

Email:

Username:

Date/Password:

Date/Password:

Date/Password:

Notes:

Website:

Email:

Username:

Date/Password:

Date/Password:

Date/Password:

Notes:

Website:

Email:

Username:

Date/Password:

Date/Password:

Date/Password:

Notes:

Website:

Email:

Username:

Date/Password:

Date/Password:

Date/Password:

Notes:

Website:

Email:

Username:

Date/Password:

Date/Password:

Date/Password:

Notes:

Website:

Email:

Username:

Date/Password:

Date/Password:

Date/Password:

Notes:

Website:

Email:

Username:

Date/Password:

Date/Password:

Date/Password:

Notes:

Website:

Email:

Username:

Date/Password:

Date/Password:

Date/Password:

Notes:

Website:

Email:

Username:

Date/Password:

Date/Password:

Date/Password:

Notes:

Website:

Email:

Username:

Date/Password:

Date/Password:

Date/Password:

Notes:

Website:

Email:

Username:

Date/Password:

Date/Password:

Date/Password:

Notes:

Website:

Email:

Username:

Date/Password:

Date/Password:

Date/Password:

Notes:

Website:

Email:

Username:

Date/Password:

Date/Password:

Date/Password:

Notes:

Website:

Email:

Username:

Date/Password:

Date/Password:

Date/Password:

Notes:

Website:

Email:

Username:

Date/Password:

Date/Password:

Date/Password:

Notes:

Website: ____

Email: ____

Username: ____

Date/Password: ____

Date/Password: ____

Date/Password: ____

Notes: ____

____

Website: ____

Email: ____

Username: ____

Date/Password: ____

Date/Password: ____

Date/Password: ____

Notes: ____

____

Website: ____

Email: ____

Username: ____

Date/Password: ____

Date/Password: ____

Date/Password: ____

Notes: ____

____

Website:

Email:

Username:

Date/Password:

Date/Password:

Date/Password:

Notes:

Website:

Email:

Username:

Date/Password:

Date/Password:

Date/Password:

Notes:

Website:

Email:

Username:

Date/Password:

Date/Password:

Date/Password:

Notes:

Website:

Email:

Username:

Date/Password:

Date/Password:

Date/Password:

Notes:

Website:

Email:

Username:

Date/Password:

Date/Password:

Date/Password:

Notes:

Webslte:

Email:

Username:

Date/Password:

Date/Password:

Date/Password:

Notes:

B

C

Website: _______________________

Email: _______________________

Username: _______________________

Date/Password: _______________________

Date/Password: _______________________

Date/Password: _______________________

Notes: _______________________

____

Website: _______________________

Email: _______________________

Username: _______________________

Date/Password: _______________________

Date/Password: _______________________

Date/Password: _______________________

Notes: _______________________

____

Website: _______________________

Email: _______________________

Username: _______________________

Date/Password: _______________________

Date/Password: _______________________

Date/Password: _______________________

Notes: _______________________

____

Website:

Email:

Username:

Date/Password:

Date/Password:

Date/Password:

Notes:

Website:

Email:

Username:

Date/Password:

Date/Password:

Date/Password:

Notes:

Website:

Email:

Username:

Date/Password:

Date/Password:

Date/Password:

Notes:

C

Website:

Email:

Username:

Date/Password:

Date/Password:

Date/Password:

Notes:

Website:

Email:

Username:

Date/Password:

Date/Password:

Date/Password:

Notes:

Website:

Email:

Username:

Date/Password:

Date/Password:

Date/Password:

Notes:

Website:

Email:

Username:

Date/Password:

Date/Password:

Date/Password:

Notes:

Website:

Email:

Username:

Date/Password:

Date/Password:

Date/Password:

Notes:

Website:

Email:

Username:

Date/Password:

Date/Password:

Date/Password:

Notes:

Website:

Email:

Username:

Date/Password:

Date/Password:

Date/Password:

Notes:

Website:

Email:

Username:

Date/Password:

Date/Password:

Date/Password:

Notes:

Website:

Email:

Username:

Date/Password:

Date/Password:

Date/Password:

Notes:

Website:

Email:

Username:

Date/Password:

Date/Password:

Date/Password:

Notes:

Website:

Email:

Username:

Date/Password:

Date/Password:

Date/Password:

Notes:

Website:

Email:

Username:

Date/Password:

Date/Password:

Date/Password:

Notes:

D

Website: ___________________________
Email: ___________________________
Username: ___________________________
Date/Password: ___________________________
Date/Password: ___________________________
Date/Password: ___________________________
Notes: ___________________________
____

Website: ___________________________
Email: ___________________________
Username: ___________________________
Date/Password: ___________________________
Date/Password: ___________________________
Date/Password: ___________________________
Notes: ___________________________
____

Website: ___________________________
Email: ___________________________
Username: ___________________________
Date/Password: ___________________________
Date/Password: ___________________________
Date/Password: ___________________________
Notes: ___________________________
____

Website:_______________________________________

Email:____

Username:______________________________________

Date/Password:_________________________________

Date/Password:_________________________________

Date/Password:_________________________________

Notes:____

____

D

Website:_______________________________________

Email:____

Username:______________________________________

Date/Password:_________________________________

Date/Password:_________________________________

Date/Password:_________________________________

Notes:____

____

Website:_______________________________________

Email:____

Username:______________________________________

Date/Password:_________________________________

Date/Password:_________________________________

Date/Password:_________________________________

Notes:____

____

E

Website:

Email:

Username:

Date/Password:

Date/Password:

Date/Password:

Notes:

Website:

Email:

Username:

Date/Password:

Date/Password:

Date/Password:

Notes:

Website:

Email:

Username:

Date/Password:

Date/Password:

Date/Password:

Notes:

Website: _______________________________________

Email: ____

Username: ______________________________________

Date/Password: _________________________________

Date/Password: _________________________________

Date/Password: _________________________________

Notes: ____

____

Website: _______________________________________

Email: ____

Username: ______________________________________

Date/Password: _________________________________

Date/Password: _________________________________

Date/Password: _________________________________

Notes: ____

____

Website: _______________________________________

Email: ____

Username: ______________________________________

Date/Password: _________________________________

Date/Password: _________________________________

Date/Password: _________________________________

Notes: ____

____

E

Website: ____

Email: ____

Username: ____

Date/Password: ____

Date/Password: ____

Date/Password: ____

Notes: ____

____

Website: ____

Email: ____

Username: ____

Date/Password: ____

Date/Password: ____

Date/Password: ____

Notes: ____

____

Website: ____

Email: ____

Username: ____

Date/Password: ____

Date/Password: ____

Date/Password: ____

Notes: ____

____

Website:

Email:

Username:

Date/Password:

Date/Password:

Date/Password:

Notes:

Website:

Email:

Username:

Date/Password:

Date/Password:

Date/Password:

Notes:

Website:

Email:

Username:

Date/Password:

Date/Password:

Date/Password:

Notes:

F

Website:

Email:

Username:

Date/Password:

Date/Password:

Date/Password:

Notes:

Website:

Email:

Username:

Date/Password:

Date/Password:

Date/Password:

Notes:

Website:

Email:

Username:

Date/Password:

Date/Password:

Date/Password:

Notes:

Website:

Email:

Username:

Date/Password:

Date/Password:

Date/Password:

Notes:

Website:

Email:

Username:

Date/Password:

Date/Password:

Date/Password:

Notes:

Website:

Email:

Username:

Date/Password:

Date/Password:

Date/Password:

Notes:

Website:____

Email:____

Username:_______________________________________

Date/Password:__________________________________

Date/Password:__________________________________

Date/Password:__________________________________

Notes:____

____

Website:____

Email:____

Username:_______________________________________

Date/Password:__________________________________

Date/Password:__________________________________

Date/Password:__________________________________

Notes:____

____

Website:____

Email:____

Username:_______________________________________

Date/Password:__________________________________

Date/Password:__________________________________

Date/Password:__________________________________

Notes:____

____

Website:

Email:

Username:

Date/Password:

Date/Password:

Date/Password:

Notes:

F

Website:

Email:

Username:

Date/Password:

Date/Password:

Date/Password:

Notes:

Website:

Email:

Username:

Date/Password:

Date/Password:

Date/Password:

Notes:

G

Website: ____
Email: ____
Username: ____
Date/Password: ____
Date/Password: ____
Date/Password: ____
Notes: ____
____

Website: ____
Email: ____
Username: ____
Date/Password: ____
Date/Password: ____
Date/Password: ____
Notes: ____
____

Website: ____
Email: ____
Username: ____
Date/Password: ____
Date/Password: ____
Date/Password: ____
Notes: ____
____

Website:

Email:

Username:

Date/Password:

Date/Password:

Date/Password:

Notes:

G

Website:

Email:

Username:

Date/Password:

Date/Password:

Date/Password:

Notes:

Website:

Email:

Username:

Date/Password:

Date/Password:

Date/Password:

Notes:

Website:
Email:
Username:
Date/Password:
Date/Password:
Date/Password:
Notes:

Website:
Email:
Username:
Date/Password:
Date/Password:
Date/Password:
Notes:

Website:
Email:
Username:
Date/Password:
Date/Password:
Date/Password:
Notes:

Website:

Email:

Username:

Date/Password:

Date/Password:

Date/Password:

Notes:

G

Website:

Email:

Username:

Date/Password:

Date/Password:

Date/Password:

Notes:

Website:

Email:

Username:

Date/Password:

Date/Password:

Date/Password:

Notes:

Website:____

Email:____

Username:____

Date/Password:____

Date/Password:____

Date/Password:____

Notes:____

____

Website:____

Email:____

Username:____

Date/Password:____

Date/Password:____

Date/Password:____

Notes:____

____

Website:____

Email:____

Username:____

Date/Password:____

Date/Password:____

Date/Password:____

Notes:____

____

Website:____

Email:____

Username:____

Date/Password:_____________________________________

Date/Password:_____________________________________

Date/Password:_____________________________________

Notes:____

____

Website:____

Email:____

Username:____

Date/Password:_____________________________________

Date/Password:_____________________________________

Date/Password:_____________________________________

Notes:____

____

Website:____

Email:____

Username:____

Date/Password:_____________________________________

Date/Password:_____________________________________

Date/Password:_____________________________________

Notes:____

____

Website:

Email:

Username:

Date/Password:

Date/Password:

Date/Password:

Notes:

Website:

Email:

Username:

Date/Password:

Date/Password:

Date/Password:

Notes:

Website:

Email:

Username:

Date/Password:

Date/Password:

Date/Password:

Notes:

Website:

Email:

Username:

Date/Password:

Date/Password:

Date/Password:

Notes:

Website:

Email:

Username:

Date/Password:

Date/Password:

Date/Password:

Notes:

Website:

Email:

Username:

Date/Password:

Date/Password:

Date/Password:

Notes:

Website:

Email:

Username:

Date/Password:

Date/Password:

Date/Password:

Notes:

Website:

Email:

Username:

Date/Password:

Date/Password:

Date/Password:

Notes:

Website:

Email:

Username:

Date/Password:

Date/Password:

Date/Password:

Notes:

Website:

Email:

Username:

Date/Password:

Date/Password:

Date/Password:

Notes:

Website:

Email:

Username:

Date/Password:

Date/Password:

Date/Password:

Notes:

Website:

Email:

Username:

Date/Password:

Date/Password:

Date/Password:

Notes:

Website:

Email:

Username:

Date/Password:

Date/Password:

Date/Password:

Notes:

Website:

Email:

Username:

Date/Password:

Date/Password:

Date/Password:

Notes:

Website:

Email:

Username:

Date/Password:

Date/Password:

Date/Password:

Notes:

Website:

Email:

Username:

Date/Password:

Date/Password:

Date/Password:

Notes:

Website:

Email:

Username:

Date/Password:

Date/Password:

Date/Password:

Notes:

Website:

Email:

Username:

Date/Password:

Date/Password:

Date/Password:

Notes:

Website: _______________________________
Email: _______________________________
Username: _______________________________
Date/Password: _______________________________
Date/Password: _______________________________
Date/Password: _______________________________
Notes: _______________________________
____

Website: _______________________________
Email: _______________________________
Username: _______________________________
Date/Password: _______________________________
Date/Password: _______________________________
Date/Password: _______________________________
Notes: _______________________________
____

Website: _______________________________
Email: _______________________________
Username: _______________________________
Date/Password: _______________________________
Date/Password: _______________________________
Date/Password: _______________________________
Notes: _______________________________
____

Website:

Email:

Username:

Date/Password:

Date/Password:

Date/Password:

Notes:

Website: J

Email:

Username:

Date/Password:

Date/Password:

Date/Password:

Notes:

Website:

Email:

Username:

Date/Password:

Date/Password:

Date/Password:

Notes:

Website:

Email:

Username:

Date/Password:

Date/Password:

Date/Password:

Notes:

J

Website:

Email:

Username:

Date/Password:

Date/Password:

Date/Password:

Notes:

Website:

Email:

Username:

Date/Password:

Date/Password:

Date/Password:

Notes:

Website:

Email:

Username:

Date/Password:

Date/Password:

Date/Password:

Notes:

Website:

Email:

Username:

Date/Password:

Date/Password:

Date/Password:

Notes:

Website:

Email:

Username:

Date/Password:

Date/Password:

Date/Password:

Notes:

Website:

Email:

Username:

Date/Password:

Date/Password:

Date/Password:

Notes:

Website:

Email:

Username:

Date/Password:

Date/Password:

Date/Password:

Notes:

Website:

Email:

Username:

Date/Password:

Date/Password:

Date/Password:

Notes:

Website:

Email:

Username:

Date/Password:

Date/Password:

Date/Password:

Notes:

Website:

Email:

Username:

Date/Password:

Date/Password:

Date/Password:

Notes:

Website:

Email:

Username:

Date/Password:

Date/Password:

Date/Password:

Notes:

Website:

Email:

Username:

Date/Password:

Date/Password:

Date/Password:

Notes:

Website:

Email:

Username:

Date/Password:

Date/Password:

Date/Password:

Notes:

Website:

Email:

Username:

Date/Password:

Date/Password:

Date/Password:

Notes:

Website:

Email:

Username:

Date/Password:

Date/Password:

Date/Password:

Notes:

Website:

Email:

Username:

Date/Password:

Date/Password:

Date/Password:

Notes:

Website:

Email:

Username:

Date/Password:

Date/Password:

Date/Password:

Notes:

Website:

Email:

Username:

Date/Password:

Date/Password:

Date/Password:

Notes:

Website:

Email:

Username:

Date/Password:

Date/Password:

Date/Password:

Notes:

Website:

Email:

Username:

Date/Password:

Date/Password:

Date/Password:

Notes:

Website:

Email:

Username:

Date/Password:

Date/Password:

Date/Password:

Notes:

Website:

Email:

Username:

Date/Password:

Date/Password:

Date/Password:

Notes:

Webslte:

Email:

Username:

Date/Password:

Date/Password:

Date/Password:

Notes:

Website:

Email:

Username:

Date/Password:

Date/Password:

Date/Password:

Notes:

Website:

Email:

Username:

Date/Password:

Date/Password:

Date/Password:

Notes:

Website:

Email:

Username:

Date/Password:

Date/Password:

Date/Password:

Notes:

Website:_______________________________

Email:_______________________________

Username:_______________________________

Date/Password:_______________________________

Date/Password:_______________________________

Date/Password:_______________________________

Notes:_______________________________

____

Website:_______________________________

Email:_______________________________

Username:_______________________________

Date/Password:_______________________________

Date/Password:_______________________________

Date/Password:_______________________________

Notes:_______________________________

____

Website:_______________________________

Email:_______________________________

Username:_______________________________

Date/Password:_______________________________

Date/Password:_______________________________

Date/Password:_______________________________

Notes:_______________________________

____

M

Website:

Email:

Username:

Date/Password:

Date/Password:

Date/Password:

Notes:

Website:

Email:

Username:

Date/Password:

Date/Password:

Date/Password:

Notes:

Website:

Email:

Username:

Date/Password:

Date/Password:

Date/Password:

Notes:

Website:

Email:

Username:

Date/Password:

Date/Password:

Date/Password:

Notes:

Website:

Email:

Username:

Date/Password:

Date/Password:

Date/Password:

Notes:

Website:

Email:

Username:

Date/Password:

Date/Password:

Date/Password:

Notes:

Website:

Email:

Username:

Date/Password:

Date/Password:

Date/Password:

Notes:

Website:

Email:

Username:

Date/Password:

Date/Password:

Date/Password:

Notes:

Website:

Email:

Username:

Date/Password:

Date/Password:

Date/Password:

Notes:

Website:

Email:

Username:

Date/Password:

Date/Password:

Date/Password:

Notes:

Website:

Email:

Username:

Date/Password:

Date/Password:

Date/Password:

Notes:

Website:

Email:

Username:

Date/Password:

Date/Password:

Date/Password:

Notes:

Website:

Email:

Username:

Date/Password:

Date/Password:

Date/Password:

Notes:

Website:

Email:

Username:

Date/Password:

Date/Password:

Date/Password:

Notes:

Website:

Email:

Username:

Date/Password:

Date/Password:

Date/Password:

Notes:

Website:

Email:

Username:

Date/Password:

Date/Password:

Date/Password:

Notes:

Website:

Email:

Username:

Date/Password:

Date/Password:

Date/Password:

Notes:

Website:

Email:

Username:

Date/Password:

Date/Password:

Date/Password:

Notes:

Website:

Email:

Username:

Date/Password:

Date/Password:

Date/Password:

Notes:

Website:

Email:

Username:

Date/Password:

Date/Password:

Date/Password:

Notes:

Website:

Email:

Username:

Date/Password:

Date/Password:

Date/Password:

Notes:

Website:

Email:

Username:

Date/Password:

Date/Password:

Date/Password:

Notes:

Website:

Email:

Username:

Date/Password:

Date/Password:

Date/Password:

Notes:

Website:

Email:

Username:

Date/Password:

Date/Password:

Date/Password:

Notes:

Website:

Email:

Username:

Date/Password:

Date/Password:

Date/Password:

Notes:

Website:

Email:

Username:

Date/Password:

Date/Password:

Date/Password:

Notes:

Website:

Email:

Username:

Date/Password:

Date/Password:

Date/Password:

Notes:

Website:

Email:

Username:

Date/Password:

Date/Password:

Date/Password:

Notes:

Website:

Email:

Username:

Date/Password:

Date/Password:

Date/Password:

Notes:

Website:

Email:

Username:

Date/Password:

Date/Password:

Date/Password:

Notes:

Website:

Email:

Username:

Date/Password:

Date/Password:

Date/Password:

Notes:

Website:

Email:

Username:

Date/Password:

Date/Password:

Date/Password:

Notes:

Website:

Email:

Username:

Date/Password:

Date/Password:

Date/Password:

Notes:

Website:

Email:

Username:

Date/Password:

Date/Password:

Date/Password:

Notes:

Website:

Email:

Username:

Date/Password:

Date/Password:

Date/Password:

Notes:

Website:

Email:

Username:

Date/Password:

Date/Password:

Date/Password:

Notes:

Website:

Email:

Username:

Date/Password:

Date/Password:

Date/Password:

Notes:

Website:

Email:

Username:

Date/Password:

Date/Password:

Date/Password:

Notes:

Website:

Email:

Username:

Date/Password:

Date/Password:

Date/Password:

Notes:

Website:

Email:

Username:

Date/Password:

Date/Password:

Date/Password:

Notes:

Website:

Email:

Username:

Date/Password:

Date/Password:

Date/Password:

Notes:

Website:

Email:

Username:

Date/Password:

Date/Password:

Date/Password:

Notes:

Website: ____

Email: ____

Username: _______________________________________

Date/Password: __________________________________

Date/Password: __________________________________

Date/Password: __________________________________

Notes: ____

____

Website: ____

Email: ____

Username: _______________________________________

Date/Password: __________________________________

Date/Password: __________________________________

Date/Password: __________________________________

Notes: ____

____

Website: ____

Email: ____

Username: _______________________________________

Date/Password: __________________________________

Date/Password: __________________________________

Date/Password: __________________________________

Notes: ____

____

Website:

Email:

Username:

Date/Password:

Date/Password:

Date/Password:

Notes:

Website:

Email:

Username:

Date/Password:

Date/Password:

Date/Password:

Notes:

Website:

Email:

Username:

Date/Password:

Date/Password:

Date/Password:

Notes:

Website:

Email:

Username:

Date/Password:

Date/Password:

Date/Password:

Notes:

Website:

Email:

Username:

Date/Password:

Date/Password:

Date/Password:

Notes:

Website:

Email:

Username:

Date/Password:

Date/Password:

Date/Password:

Notes:

Website:

Email:

Username:

Date/Password:

Date/Password:

Date/Password:

Notes:

Website:

Email:

Username:

Date/Password:

Date/Password:

Date/Password:

Notes:

Website:

Email:

Username:

Date/Password:

Date/Password:

Date/Password:

Notes:

Website:

Email:

Username:

Date/Password:

Date/Password:

Date/Password:

Notes:

Website:

Email:

Username:

Date/Password:

Date/Password:

Date/Password:

Notes:

Website:

Email:

Username:

Date/Password:

Date/Password:

Date/Password:

Notes:

Website:

Email:

Username:

Date/Password:

Date/Password:

Date/Password:

Notes:

Website:

Email:

Username:

Date/Password:

Date/Password:

Date/Password:

Notes:

R

Website:

Email:

Username:

Date/Password:

Date/Password:

Date/Password:

Notes:

Website:

Email:

Username:

Date/Password:

Date/Password:

Date/Password:

Notes:

Website:

Email:

Username:

Date/Password:

Date/Password:

Date/Password:

Notes:

Website:

Email:

Username:

Date/Password:

Date/Password:

Date/Password:

Notes:

R

Website: ___________________________
Email: _____________________________
Username: __________________________
Date/Password: _____________________
Date/Password: _____________________
Date/Password: _____________________
Notes: _____________________________
____

Website: ___________________________
Email: _____________________________
Username: __________________________
Date/Password: _____________________
Date/Password: _____________________
Date/Password: _____________________
Notes: _____________________________
____

Website: ___________________________
Email: _____________________________
Username: __________________________
Date/Password: _____________________
Date/Password: _____________________
Date/Password: _____________________
Notes: _____________________________
____

Website:

Email:

Username:

Date/Password:

Date/Password:

Date/Password:

Notes:

Website:

Email:

Username:

Date/Password:

Date/Password:

Date/Password:

Notes:

Website:

Email:

Username:

Date/Password:

Date/Password:

Date/Password:

Notes:

| Website: |
| Email: |
| Username: |
| Date/Password: |
| Date/Password: |
| Date/Password: |
| Notes: |

| Website: |
| Email: |
| Username: |
| Date/Password: |
| Date/Password: |
| Date/Password: |
| Notes: |

| Website: |
| Email: |
| Username: |
| Date/Password: |
| Date/Password: |
| Date/Password: |
| Notes: |

Website:

Email:

Username:

Date/Password:

Date/Password:

Date/Password:

Notes:

Website:

Email:

Username:

Date/Password:

Date/Password:

Date/Password:

Notes:

Website:

Email:

Username:

Date/Password:

Date/Password:

Date/Password:

Notes:

S

Website:

Email:

Username:

Date/Password:

Date/Password:

Date/Password:

Notes:

Website:

Email:

Username:

Date/Password:

Date/Password:

Date/Password:

Notes:

Website:

Email:

Username:

Date/Password:

Date/Password:

Date/Password:

Notes:

Website:

Email:

Username:

Date/Password:

Date/Password:

Date/Password:

Notes:

Website:

Email:

Username:

Date/Password:

Date/Password:

Date/Password:

Notes:

Website:

Email:

Username:

Date/Password:

Date/Password:

Date/Password:

Notes:

Website:

Email:

Username:

Date/Password:

Date/Password:

Date/Password:

Notes:

Website:

Email:

Username:

Date/Password:

Date/Password:

Date/Password:

Notes:

Website:

Email:

Username:

Date/Password:

Date/Password:

Date/Password:

Notes:

Website:

Email:

Username:

Date/Password:

Date/Password:

Date/Password:

Notes:

Website:

Email:

Username:

Date/Password:

Date/Password:

Date/Password:

Notes:

Website:

Email:

Username:

Date/Password:

Date/Password:

Date/Password:

Notes:

Website:

Email:

Username:

Date/Password:

Date/Password:

Date/Password:

Notes:

Website:

Email:

Username:

Date/Password:

Date/Password:

Date/Password:

Notes:

Website:

Email:

Username:

Date/Password:

Date/Password:

Date/Password:

Notes:

Website:

Email:

Username:

Date/Password:

Date/Password:

Date/Password:

Notes:

Website:

Email:

Username:

Date/Password:

Date/Password:

Date/Password:

Notes:

Website:

Email:

Username:

Date/Password:

Date/Password:

Date/Password:

Notes:

Website:

Email:

Username:

Date/Password:

Date/Password:

Date/Password:

Notes:

Website:

Email:

Username:

Date/Password:

Date/Password:

Date/Password:

Notes:

Website:

Email:

Username:

Date/Password:

Date/Password:

Date/Password:

Notes:

Website:

Email:

Username:

Date/Password:

Date/Password:

Date/Password:

Notes:

Website:

Email:

Username:

Date/Password:

Date/Password:

Date/Password:

Notes:

Website:

Email:

Username:

Date/Password:

Date/Password:

Date/Password:

Notes:

Website: _______________________

Email: _________________________

Username: ______________________

Date/Password: _________________

Date/Password: _________________

Date/Password: _________________

Notes: _________________________

____

Website: _______________________

Email: _________________________

Username: ______________________

Date/Password: _________________

Date/Password: _________________

Date/Password: _________________

Notes: _________________________

____

Website: _______________________

Email: _________________________

Username: ______________________

Date/Password: _________________

Date/Password: _________________

Date/Password: _________________

Notes: _________________________

____

Website:

Email:

Username:

Date/Password:

Date/Password:

Date/Password:

Notes:

Website:

Email:

Username:

Date/Password:

Date/Password:

Date/Password:

Notes:

Website:

Email:

Username:

Date/Password:

Date/Password:

Date/Password:

Notes:

U

Website:

Email:

Username:

Date/Password:

Date/Password:

Date/Password:

Notes:

Website:

Email:

Username:

Date/Password:

Date/Password:

Date/Password:

Notes:

Website:

Email:

Username:

Date/Password:

Date/Password:

Date/Password:

Notes:

Website:

Email:

Username:

Date/Password:

Date/Password:

Date/Password:

Notes:

Website:

Email:

Username:

Date/Password:

Date/Password:

Date/Password:

Notes:

Website:

Email:

Username:

Date/Password:

Date/Password:

Date/Password:

Notes:

Website:

Email:

Username:

Date/Password:

Date/Password:

Date/Password:

Notes:

Website:

Email:

Username:

Date/Password:

Date/Password:

Date/Password:

Notes:

Website:

Email:

Username:

Date/Password:

Date/Password:

Date/Password:

Notes:

Website:

Email:

Username:

Date/Password:

Date/Password:

Date/Password:

Notes:

Website:

Email:

Username:

Date/Password:

Date/Password:

Date/Password:

Notes:

Website:

Email:

Username:

Date/Password:

Date/Password:

Date/Password:

Notes:

V

Website:

Email:

Username:

Date/Password:

Date/Password:

Date/Password:

Notes:

Website:

Email:

Username:

Date/Password:

Date/Password:

Date/Password:

Notes:

Website:

Email:

Username:

Date/Password:

Date/Password:

Date/Password:

Notes:

Website:_______________________________________

Email:____

Username:______________________________________

Date/Password:_________________________________

Date/Password:_________________________________

Date/Password:_________________________________

Notes:____

____

Website:_______________________________________

Email:____

Username:______________________________________

Date/Password:_________________________________

Date/Password:_________________________________

Date/Password:_________________________________

Notes:____

____

Website:_______________________________________

Email:____

Username:______________________________________

Date/Password:_________________________________

Date/Password:_________________________________

Date/Password:_________________________________

Notes:____

____

Website: ____

Email: ____

Username: ____

Date/Password: _____________________________________

Date/Password: _____________________________________

Date/Password: _____________________________________

Notes: ____

____

Website: ____

Email: ____

Username: ____

Date/Password: _____________________________________

Date/Password: _____________________________________

Date/Password: _____________________________________

Notes: ____

____

Website: ____

Email: ____

Username: ____

Date/Password: _____________________________________

Date/Password: _____________________________________

Date/Password: _____________________________________

Notes: ____

____

Website:

Email:

Username:

Date/Password:

Date/Password:

Date/Password:

Notes:

Website:

Email:

Username:

Date/Password:

Date/Password:

Date/Password:

Notes:

Website:

Email:

Username:

Date/Password:

Date/Password:

Date/Password:

Notes:

Website:

Email:

Username:

Date/Password:

Date/Password:

Date/Password:

Notes:

Website:

Email:

Username:

Date/Password:

Date/Password:

Date/Password:

Notes:

Website:

Email:

Username:

Date/Password:

Date/Password:

Date/Password:

Notes:

Website:

Email:

Username:

Date/Password:

Date/Password:

Date/Password:

Notes:

Website:

Email:

Username:

Date/Password:

Date/Password:

Date/Password:

Notes:

Website:

Email:

Username:

Date/Password:

Date/Password:

Date/Password:

Notes:

Website:

Email:

Username:

Date/Password:

Date/Password:

Date/Password:

Notes:

Website:

Email:

Username:

Date/Password:

Date/Password:

Date/Password:

Notes:

Website:

Email:

Username:

Date/Password:

Date/Password:

Date/Password:

Notes:

Website:____

Email:____

Username:____

Date/Password:____

Date/Password:____

Date/Password:____

Notes:____

____

Website.____

Email:____

Username:____

Date/Password:____

Date/Password:____

Date/Password:____

Notes:____

____

Website:____

Email:____

Username:____

Date/Password:____

Date/Password:____

Date/Password:____

Notes:____

____

Website: ___________________________

Email: ___________________________

Username: ___________________________

Date/Password: ___________________________

Date/Password: ___________________________

Date/Password: ___________________________

Notes: ___________________________

____

Website: ___________________________

Email: ___________________________

Username: ___________________________

Date/Password: ___________________________

Date/Password: ___________________________

Date/Password: ___________________________

Notes: ___________________________

____

Website: ___________________________

Email: ___________________________

Username: ___________________________

Date/Password: ___________________________

Date/Password: ___________________________

Date/Password: ___________________________

Notes: ___________________________

____

Website:

Email:

Username:

Date/Password:

Date/Password:

Date/Password:

Notes:

Website:

Email:

Username:

Date/Password:

Date/Password:

Date/Password:

Notes:

Website:

Email:

Username:

Date/Password:

Date/Password:

Date/Password:

Notes:

Website:

Email:

Username:

Date/Password:

Date/Password:

Date/Password:

Notes:

Website:

Email:

Username:

Date/Password:

Date/Password:

Date/Password:

Notes:

Website:

Email:

Username:

Date/Password:

Date/Password:

Date/Password:

Notes:

Website:

Email:

Username:

Date/Password:

Date/Password:

Date/Password:

Notes:

Website:

Email:

Username:

Date/Password:

Date/Password:

Date/Password:

Notes:

Website:

Email:

Username:

Date/Password:

Date/Password:

Date/Password:

Notes:

Website:

Email:

Username:

Date/Password:

Date/Password:

Date/Password:

Notes:

Website:

Email:

Username:

Date/Password:

Date/Password:

Date/Password:

Notes:

Website:

Email:

Username:

Date/Password:

Date/Password:

Date/Password:

Notes:

Website:

Email:

Username:

Date/Password:

Date/Password:

Date/Password:

Notes:

Website:

Email:

Username:

Date/Password:

Date/Password:

Date/Password:

Notes:

Website:

Email:

Username:

Date/Password:

Date/Password:

Date/Password:

Notes:

Z

Website:

Email:

Username:

Date/Password:

Date/Password:

Date/Password:

Notes:

Website:

Email:

Username:

Date/Password:

Date/Password:

Date/Password:

Notes:

Website:

Email:

Username:

Date/Password:

Date/Password:

Date/Password:

Notes:

Website:

Email:

Username:

Date/Password:

Date/Password:

Date/Password:

Notes:

Website:

Email:

Username:

Date/Password:

Date/Password:

Date/Password:

Notes:

Website:

Email:

Username:

Date/Password:

Date/Password:

Date/Password:

Notes:

NOTES

NOTES

Made in the USA
Monee, IL
07 July 2026

56550097R00066